POEMS F

POEMS FROM THE HEART

Tina Cashmore

ARTHUR H. STOCKWELL LTD.
Torrs Park   Ilfracombe   Devon
Established 1898
www.ahstockwell.co.uk

© Tina Cashmore, 2003
First published in Great Britain, 2003
All rights reserved.
*No part of this publication may be reproduced
or transmitted in any form or by any means,
electronic or mechanical, including photocopy,
recording, or any information storage and
retrieval system, without permission
in writing from the copyright holder.*

*British Library Cataloguing-in-Publication Data.
A catalogue record for this book is available
from the British Library.*

*ISBN 0 7223 3403-6
Printed in Great Britain by
Arthur H. Stockwell Ltd.
Torrs Park   Ilfracombe
Devon*

I dedicate this book to my husband Nicholas
and daughter Jessica, who have made my
life so happy and have supported me and
inspired me to write this book.
I love you both so much, *Tina.*

Contents

Good Morning Sunshine	13
Today	14
The Stars	15
Cheer Up	16
The Beginning	17
The Wishing Well	18
Touched by an Angel	19
Our Second Life	20
The Dove	21
My Invisible Friend Kate	22
What If?	23
My Perfect Dreams	24
The New Millennium	25
The Tramp	26
A Bedtime Story	27
Mindy and Me	28
The Butterfly	30
When God Forgot to Teach	31
Grandad (Grampy)	32
The Dark	34

The Barn Owl	35
Children Playing	36
A Farmer's Prayer	37
The Rainbow	38
Wild Things	39
Tomorrow	40
The Birds	41
Let's Dance	42
The Sea	43
Springtime	44
My Special Mother	45
Hello Mister Clown	46
Any Time You Need a Friend	47
The Meaning of Love	48
A Perfect Day	49
The Breeze	50
Shed Your Tears	51
The Snowman	52
Superstition	53
The Two of Us	54
The Rain	55

Yesterday	56
Equal Rights	57
A Penny For Your Thoughts	58
The Christmas Presents	59
The Four Seasons	60
A Loving Dog	61
My Mother's Words	62
Baby Liam	64
The Eternal World	66
The Comforts of Home	67
That Loving Feeling	68
Lord	69
The Ballerina	70
The Frost	71
Picking the Fruits	72
Our Special Song	73
Our Special Love	74
The Short Life	76
The Children's Riddle	78
Never a Doubt	79

Good Morning Sunshine

Pulling back the kitchen curtain,
You're shining through so bright;
Today, I feel a wonderful day,
As you're shining down your light.

The warmth you're shining down at me,
Is touching me inside;
I feel a smile upon my face,
A smile to show with pride.

And now, dear sunshine you are awake,
As you glow bright, with heat you bake;
Everyone's happy, the children they play,
The air is fresh; what a beautiful day.

Today

Today, it is another day,
Tomorrow comes too fast;
The years they go so quickly by,
But the memories will always last.

Today, it is another day,
What it holds, we do not know;
As every minute passes by,
Our intelligence will only grow.

For today is different in every way,
From the one we had before;
Soon it will be tomorrow,
We will learn that little bit more.

The Stars

All alone, I look at you,
Shining bright, what do you do?
You look so near, yet far away,
A world of mysteries, what can I say?

If only you could talk to us,
And tell us what you hold,
A secret key to all our lives,
A world of yet unknowns.

As I look up, and start to dream,
The things I wish could be;
Through all the troubles I may have,
You're shining down on me.

Cheer Up

Hold your head high and never look down,
Put a smile on your face and never a frown,
For if you feel sad, just think of the past,
All the happier days, the memories that last.

For never feel lonely, never feel sad,
Always think of the good, and never the bad;
Tomorrow will come, a new day is near,
Let us not weep, cry only a cheer.

Life is too precious to live in such pain,
Always be happy, but never in vain;
A new day nears, the brightness in sight,
Never give in, don't give up that fight.

The Beginning

Did God create the human race,
Or did we fall from outer space?
How did we start? How will we end?
Are we here with a message to send?

There's many a thing we'll never know,
Why we're here and why we go.
Questions unanswered, they'll always be;
Our lives, they are a mystery.

If only we could relive the start,
To see how it all began,
Then we'd change a lot of things,
And learn to live with man.

The Wishing Well

Throw your pennies in the well,
Make a wish, don't cast a spell;
Keep your wish all to yourself,
Dream of it and dream of wealth.

The wish will keep your hopes alive,
To see if it comes true;
And if it does, good wishing well,
It's all because of you.

Touched by an Angel

My mom she was so really ill,
Blood seeped in her brain;
She only had two days to live,
But then the angels came.

I'm glad she's had a second chance,
At the age of fifty-four;
The angels heard my cry for help,
Came knocking at my door.

Until now, I wasn't so sure,
If angels were so real;
But now I have my mother back,
Their presence I can feel.

Thank you angels for hearing my cry,
You saved her life, not let her die;
I'll always be grateful to you up above,
For bringing her back, the mother I love.

Dedicated to my very special mother, Yvonne.

Our Second Life

There's said to be another life,
From this that we now hold;
A ray of light that waits for us,
To go when we are told.

For when we part this life we lead,
That we no longer have to feed;
To join the others we've lost before,
Our day will come, we'll have that call.

They say it is a better place,
For all of us to be;
A place so peaceful, filled with love,
And live in harmony.

The Dove

Open your wings and spread us some peace,
Fly over our heads and purity release;
Spread us some peace and always be near,
Let us live happy and never in fear.

For you are a symbol of many a thing,
Purity, peace and love;
You are the rarest of them all,
We watch you up above.

Fly up high and spread all the good,
Give us new hope, let us be understood;
A symbol of peace you certainly are,
Stay close to our hearts and never go far.

My Invisible Friend Kate

When I was just a little girl
I liked to play 'Pretend',
That Kate was playing with me;
She was my invisible friend.

I always used to tell her off,
She'd think that I was mad;
Then I'd see her look at me,
A look that was real sad.

I always used to talk to her,
And pretend she was at my side,
Playing dolls and puzzles too,
Or going down the slide.

I often sit alone right now,
And wonder what Kate would say,
If she could see how grown I am,
And happy in every way.

What If?

No more wars, poverty or neglect,
Children safe, races uniting,
People together, no more fighting;
What a wonderful world it would be.

Imagine everything in its place,
With happiness, love and laughter;
What a wonderful life it would be,
If we all lived happy ever after.

To stop the cruelty, that is the task,
To make the best things longer last;
If we all took a part, opened our eyes to see,
What a wonderful world, it certainly would be.

My Perfect Dreams

As we close our eyes and go to sleep,
We dream of things to be;
Dreaming of that perfect world,
We know we'll never see.

But as we dream it gives us hope,
The things that we could change;
A perfect world, a perfect life,
The things to rearrange.

Although we know it cannot be,
Our dreams keep hopes alive;
Some dreams they often do come true,
Much later on in life.

The New Millennium

Two thousand years have now gone by,
A new millennium is here,
For we will never see again,
The day we all did cheer.

Fireworks that lit up the sky,
As the seconds passed us by;
People cheering, having fun,
A day to remember, a special one.

The celebrations of this age,
The world it all stood still;
People merry and having fun,
And showing all goodwill.

For we will never see again,
The things we saw that night;
The sky full of all colours and lights,
And dancing with delight.

The Tramp

Your clothes are threadbare,
No shoes on your feet;
You rummage in bins,
For that something to eat.

Never a look, never a word,
Your cry out for help, is always unheard.
So why do you choose this terrible life,
No one to love, not even a wife?

Never a bath, nor never a shower,
Sadness surrounds you, you hide and you cower.
Do something better, from this life you lead,
Someone is here, to help you in need.

Begging for money, no clothes on your back,
Your only possessions are in your old sack.
Pick up the pieces and face to your fears,
Let someone in, the light will appear.

A Bedtime Story

Good night our darling, off to sleep,
I pray to God, for your safe keep.
Thank you for the joy you bring,
For when you're near, our hearts they sing.

Mother's girl, and father's too,
You changed our lives from black to blue.
A special girl, you are the best,
You changed the wind from east to west.

For everyday you shine so bright,
And make our lives complete.
For all the things you do and say,
Our hearts they miss a beat.

Dedicated to my darling daughter, Jessica.

Mindy and Me

Mindy is my one true friend,
I've known since I was three;
Growing up together,
We played so happily.

Sisters we were said to be,
As we never were apart;
Playing at our houses,
When the day began to start.

Through all our lives, we did so much,
Inseparable we'd become;
All the teenage years we had,
Every day was a special one.

Though now we are both married,
We've vowed not ever to part;
Our memories will always be with us,
They'll always stay in our hearts.

There is an ending to this tale,
We've both had daughters you see,
Soon they'll grow and make a bond,
Be friends like Mindy and me.

The Butterfly

The butterfly lays its wings to rest
Upon a beautiful flower;
Beautiful colours has its wings,
Full of life and power.

Flying over our heads so peacefully,
A symbol of life and tranquillity;
Flying around without any sound,
Delicate and light, not touching the ground.

We stop to wonder, we stop to stare,
A silent presence you do so wear;
Now go fly high and touch the sky,
Forever be seen, oh beautiful fly.

When God Forgot to Teach

When God created the human race,
He forgot to put a smile on our face;
He forgot to teach us right from wrong,
He forgot to teach us to live as one.

He forgot to teach us never to starve,
He forgot to teach us there's love in our hearts;
He forgot to teach us to care for another,
He forgot to teach us to help one another.

He forgot to teach us what lies ahead,
He forgot to teach us what shouldn't be said;
He forgot to teach us never to fight,
He forgot to teach us the dark and the light.

For God, He forgot many things,
Maybe, it was just meant to be.
Are we here, or is it a dream?
We'll all have to wait and see.

Grandad (Grampy)

You were my very loving friend.
Why did you go? Why did you end?
I miss you every single day;
How much, my words they cannot say.

I wish we could have said goodbye,
Then I'd no longer need to cry.
I touched your face, now you're asleep;
Goodbye my grandad, sleep in peace.

You were a special friend to me,
A loving man, you'll always be;
I'm grateful for the times we had,
But now I feel so really sad.

Up to heaven, now you go,
Why you've gone, I'll never know;
I hope you're looking down on me,
I'll always be here for you to see.

My memories though will always last,
I never will forget the past;
There'll always be a place in me
And that's for you, my special grampy.

Dedicated to my grandad, Bill.

The Dark

Why are we afraid of the dark?
No light to be seen, not even a spark,
Nothing to touch, nothing to hold;
The dark makes us scared, timid not bold.

For we cannot see the things around,
Nothing to be seen, nor to be found;
As we feel our way to turn on the light,
Our hearts race away, so scared with the fright.

The room is not silent, for the clock ticks away,
Touching the switch puts my frightness at bay;
Soon there'll be light, darkness no more,
The dark disappears, now my feet touch the floor.

The Barn Owl

Why do you stare? Why do you glare?
Do you have something to say?
You are unique, a species so rare,
You live in a barn of hay.

You watch our every single move,
With your glowing eyes to see;
Speckled brown feathers, a big white chest,
You're looking down at me.

Still as the night, you sit on a beam,
Not knowing you are there;
In a dark corner, high up above,
Your claws are waiting to tear.

An endangered species you have become,
I'm glad that I've seen you;
Now go spread your wings, fly up in the sky,
And do what you have to do.

Children Playing

Skipping down the pathway,
The children go to play,
Talking to each other,
On a bright and sunny day.

Their happy smiling faces,
Oblivious to what's around,
Shouting and playing together;
Laughter the only sound.

A lovely sight it is to see,
Children together so happily;
Playing and laughing and having such fun,
No cares in the world, their lives just begun.

A Farmer's Prayer

When the stars are in,
The frost will fall.
When the cows lie down,
Bad weather will call.

When the weather is dry,
A good harvest will be.
When the weather is wet,
No funds will be seen.

So we pray to You Lord,
Be kind to our seeds;
Give us good weather
And tender our needs.

The Rainbow

Alive with colours, you certainly are,
You never end, yet go so far;
A pot of gold you're said to have,
When you appear, we never feel sad.

How you get there, we never know,
Your glowing colours all in a bow;
Red and yellow, pink and green,
The rain has gone, and now you so gleam.

You never last, yet never end,
Are you here, a message to send?
Our hearts miss a beat, when we look at you,
Oh, mysterious thing, in a sky full of blue.

Wild Things

What do you think? Where do you go?
You hide all day, at night you show.
You are untamed and certainly free;
You come and go, just as you please.

You do not know, any other,
For what it's like, to hurt another.
You have no worries, you're free to roam;
You come and go, in your own home.

To live my life as free as you,
Could only be a dream come true.
As free as a bird, I'd love to fly,
Living so free, not living a lie.

Tomorrow

What it holds, we do not know.
Will it go fast or will it go slow?
What will happen to us all?
Will the trees still stand so tall?

For every second of the day,
The good and bad won't go away.
Why need we mend our broken hearts?
Maybe tomorrow will be a new start?

No more sorrow, no more pain,
Only bright colours and never the rain;
Teaching each other to become as one,
I pray and hope tomorrow will come.

The Birds

Flying high up in the sky,
In a flock you pass us by;
You look so tiny, high up there,
As you fly on without a care.

You dance in the sky, so pure and so free,
Your wings spread out wide, you sparkle with glee;
Fly over the pastures onto the land,
Into a meadow, where your food can be found.

Wonderful creatures you certainly are,
With your precious wings, to take you so far;
You play in peace, in the skyline of blue,
With heaven above you, your souls are so true.

Without any troubles, you go off on your way,
Your beauty within, makes you dance all the day;
All singing in tune, a moment to treasure,
A symbol of life and your peace is forever.

Let's Dance

As we join our hands and dance away,
Our bodies so close, we begin to sway;
Close to each other, our bodies they touch,
Heads on our shoulders, not talking too much.

A moment of feeling I cannot describe,
Holding you near, so close by my side;
Dancing away to the rhythm in time,
Tears fill up, 'cause I know you are mine.

The music slows down, the record has stopped,
My heart beats so fast, feels like it's popped;
Can't wait till tomorrow, till we dance again,
The love of my life, and my special friend.

The Sea

Calm and peaceful is the sea,
A different life with tranquillity;
A world of mysteries it's said to hold,
Sunken ships, treasures and gold.

For many a thing has been lost at sea,
Years to unfold, it holds many keys;
Beautiful sea life swims on the sand,
Anchors and wrecks, all lost from this land.

A world of beauty, we cannot describe,
Sunken islands and cities, once they did rise;
Many a secret it keeps to itself,
The beautiful sea, full of riches and wealth.

Springtime

Glistening brightly is the sun,
The buds they open, one by one;
The grass grows tall, with all its might,
The birds awake, and now in flight.

New lives begin, and things they grow,
One by one the seeds we've sewn;
Up through the earth, the shoots they rise,
And soon will blossom before our eyes.

For everything is fresh and new,
The sky is now a crystal blue;
Spring is here, it's all begun,
Let's hope it is a special one.

My Special Mother

Mom, you are my very special friend,
That no one could replace;
You listen when I'm feeling down,
You certainly know your place.

Your advice and love you freely give,
You're never far away;
You're there when I am feeling down,
You listen to what I say.

Your help and love I greatly receive,
You're even there when I'm in need;
Cheering me up and helping me through,
I owe it all, all to you.

Through all the years, you've never moaned,
You made me smile, when I have groaned;
I hope you're as proud, as I am of you;
You are my soul mate, and I love you.

You've taught me everything I need to know,
Morals, rights and wrongs;
The thing that will always remain so close,
And that's our special bond.

Hello Mister Clown

A cry of laughter heard in the street,
Children are laughing at the size of your feet;
Funny illusions, the magic unwinds,
All eyes fixed on you, never looking behind.

A bright red nose and wide starry eyes,
Big baggy trousers, that rest on your thighs;
Big red lips and bright yellow hair,
That enormous big smile, can be seen anywhere.

The children are happy, you've brought so much joy,
You've pulled out the flowers, now pulled out a toy;
The children content, now happy and gay,
It certainly shows, what a wonderful day.

Sincere thanks to you Mister Clown,
The children now smiling, and not looking down;
You've made them be happy, thank you so much,
For just being you, and giving your touch.

Any Time You Need a Friend

When you are feeling lonely,
And no place left to go,
Pick up the phone and call me;
I'm someone you don't know.

For all the troubles that you have,
Never feel lonely, never feel sad;
Never think the worst of things,
Soon you'll know that you can win.

Although right now, you feel despair,
Heartache and unloved,
If you would talk to someone else,
Your troubles will lift above.

There's brighter things to your life,
For now what you do see;
Open up your heart right now,
And put your trust in me.

I am a friend you do not know,
I also feel your pain;
A listening ear, I'll talk to you,
And we'll find that light again.

Dedicated to the Samaritans.

The Meaning of Love

Love is rare, but all around,
Just like gold dust upon the ground;
Hold out your hands for others to grasp,
Teach them to love and forget all the past.

Be a pillar of strength for *all* those in need,
Teach them to love, and never with greed;
Open your hearts and let someone in,
Loving another, a new era begins.

Never a heartache, never a strife,
Teach people around, a new meaning to life;
Shout out from the rooftops high up above,
I'm happier now, 'cause I'm in love.

A Perfect Day

A perfect day, what would that be?
It's really hard to say.
A shining sun, a happy face,
The clouds would move away.

All pain has gone, and sadness too,
Our world is filled with love;
The smoke has gone and so have the fumes,
The birds will dance above.

We'd help all those who are in need,
Teaching the others who only see greed;
Mixing with races, we'd never have done,
Not giving in, until we had won.

The children a song, they so would sing,
The bells would chime out a heavenly ring;
Never a bad word, spoken that day,
All of the needy, no more turned away.

That perfect day, will it never come?
We know we'll never see,
A world so different from this one;
It would mean so much to me.

The Breeze

Softly blowing through the trees,
Not stormy wind, it is the breeze;
Blowing softly on our face,
Cooling down the human race.

For when you come, the plants they move,
Gently side to side;
As I stroll down a country lane,
Walking in my stride.

The grass moves gently on the road,
The wheat in fields too;
The living things are all content,
And all because of you.

Shed Your Tears

It's hard when you are feeling sad,
To keep your tears at bay;
You really want to cry out loud,
For you have so much to say.

For the sorrow deep inside of you,
You don't want others to see;
But if you let the tears roll down,
You'll show your agony.

Be brave and let the tears flow,
And trickle down your cheeks;
Let all the pain come out of you,
You won't be classed as weak.

It isn't shameful to shed a tear,
Everyone hurts inside;
Cry out loud, and let it out,
And begin to mend your life.

The Snowman

The snow has fallen, the weather is dry,
Let's build a snowman, ever so high;
Buttons for his eyes, carrot for his nose,
A warm woollen scarf for when the wind blows.

Reliving our childhood is what we will do,
Building a snowman, our dreams will come true;
Remembering the years, we had so much fun,
Taking a picture, when the snowman is done.

Pure white and so cold, he looks oh so real,
As we pat down the snow, our hands cannot feel;
I wish he could move and chatter to us,
Some tales to tell and dreams to discuss.

As he slowly melts before our own eyes,
Another year gone, now shorter our lives;
Let's pray the next snow will fall very soon,
Until that day, I'll just dream in my room.

Superstition

Are you superstitious,
Or don't you think it's true?
Would you go under a ladder,
Or have your palm read too?

Superstition is a funny thing,
It's said your luck will change;
For when you break a mirror,
Your life will rearrange.

A black cat crossing your path,
Bad things are said to come;
A magpie flying over,
Sorrow is said by some.

Not all bad things are said to be,
Some things are lucky too;
Finding a penny on the floor,
A lucky day for you.

Finding a four-leaf clover
Or pulling the turkey's bone;
I'll wish for all the lucky things,
To keep my happy home.

The Two of Us

We said our vows to last forever,
Through thick and thin, part we never;
Years have passed, our love has grown,
Being together is all we've known.

Through all our troubles, we carry on,
As if our lives have just begun;
Loving each other, as if just the start,
Being together and never apart.

We are two souls now joined up as one,
Laughing together and having such fun;
Husband and wife together like gold,
Rare and strong and precious to hold.

The Rain

As I look out the window,
The rain is pouring down;
Things are getting wetter,
Soaking in the ground.

Pitter-patter on the road,
The rain has come with wet and cold.
How long before it goes away?
I only wish the skies would say.

You've fed the plants, and fed the trees,
And now it's time for you to leave;
Off you go, and sun shine bright,
Give our lives a ray of light.

Yesterday

Yesterday seems so far away,
From what we did today;
For every day that passes by,
Those memories hardly stay.

For yesterday, what did we do,
And did we really care?
Each day is just a bonus;
Every day is just as rare.

And from now on, I'll take more note
Of those things I did today;
Praying that some special things,
Will soon be coming my way.

Equal Rights

Men and women are both a race,
Human in every way;
Women can do many a thing,
Throughout a normal day.

Come on men, give up your pride,
We'll show you how it's done;
Women are just as good as you,
We won't give in, till we've won.

The jobs before only men could do,
Women are now employed;
We used to be the weaker sex,
But now all that is void.

It's time to admit, you all are wrong,
And we can do just as good;
All the jobs, you classed as men's,
And told us where we stood.

We may not be as strong as you,
But we will certainly try,
To make a stand for equal rights,
And watch you swallow your pride.

A Penny For Your Thoughts

Give me a penny for your thoughts,
And tell me what you think.
Are you dreaming of today,
Or thinking of last week?

I hope your thoughts are of good things,
Which make your life content,
Or are they of some sadly things,
You'd like to make exempt?

As we think, the world stands still,
Not knowing what's around;
Thinking quietly to ourselves,
Not making any sound.

Thoughts are with us night and day,
No matter what we do;
If everyone had happy thoughts,
Our face would smile too.

The Christmas Presents

Waking up on Christmas Day,
We race to find the tree;
Underneath the branches,
Lie presents for you and me.

Shiny paper, a big red bow,
The tinsel makes the paper glow;
Look at the label, look at the tag.
Who is it from? What's in the bag?

Tearing the paper, ripping it up,
Pulling the wrapper, the sticky tape stuck;
Hurry up hands, let's see what's inside,
A beautiful dolly, will now be my pride.

The Four Seasons

The rain it falls, the wind it blows,
The sun comes out, and then it snows;
Hot or cold, wet or dry,
We say hello and then goodbye.

Spring it comes, then it's gone,
Summer comes with all the sun;
Autumn comes and brings the rain,
Winter comes, then goes again.

A Loving Dog

A family member is what you are,
A loving dog, you never go far;
A wagging tail is what you have,
You make me smile when I feel sad.

Night and day you're by my side,
You walk with me and show your pride;
When I come home you're at the door,
When I'm asleep, you're on the floor.

A special friend you are to me,
I wish that you could speak,
To tell me any troubles you have
Or when you're feeling weak.

You are a soul mate special to me,
The love you give, a rarity;
For your every need, I try to tend,
My loving dog and my best friend.

My Mother's Words

My mother always said to me,
Do the best you can,
And if you do not do that well,
I'll surely understand.

For you can only try your best,
And that is good for me;
We always will be proud of you,
In everything we see.

We cannot tell you how to live,
Your life is up to you,
But we will always give support,
In everything you do

For none of us are perfect,
But at least we'll have a try;
And if you fail in what you do,
You wave that task goodbye.

My mother always said to me,
Be happy and live your life;
Do the things that you so wish,
Go on without a strife.

But most of all she said to me,
These words will always stay;
Follow your dreams and follow your heart,
But be happy in every way.

Baby Liam

Several years of heartache
For a baby girl or boy;
So many disappointments
Longing for that joy.

The days and hours passed them by;
The clock, it ticked so slow.
Every time, another test,
The answer always no.

Giving in, they never would,
There had to be a way.
The doctors said "IMPOSSIBLE",
Give up, 'tis all they'd say.

Suddenly, the sun shone through,
A ray of light came down.
Upon their faces was a smile,
Instead of glooms and frowns.

Nine months on, Liam was born,
Our hearts they sang with joy,
To see them smiling with content,
He is a special boy.

And finally a happy tale,
Through many years of frowns;
To all of you, who long for joy,
You'll have your ups and downs.

There is a chance, there is a way,
Time is on your side;
And when that light shines down on you,
You'll smile and show your pride.

Dedicated to my brother, Adrian, and his wife, Rebecca.

The Eternal World

The world is certainly not perfect,
The world is certainly not round;
Different people all over the world,
Different sights and different sounds.

The human race united as one,
People laughing and having fun;
Imagine the love that could be found,
Not square our world, it would be round.

A perfect world and a slower pace,
Is all we ask of the human race;
To love each other, that is the task,
Our eternal world would surely last.

It's up to us, to make it true,
Let the rain never pour, but the sky be blue;
Sunshine always in our hearts
I pray tomorrow our amends will start.

The Comforts of Home

As we travel around, seeing the sights,
Boarding the plane, and off on our flights;
Soon we'll be back, home on our land,
Back to the comforts, back from the sand.

For when we're away, the days go so slow,
Missing the comforts, that we only know;
Sitting at home, watching TV,
Cooking the dinner, or eating our tea.

There is no other place like home,
For this I cannot deny;
I miss the comforts that I love,
And my family that sit by my side.

That Loving Feeling

Love will take its time to come,
It will not happen fast;
For when you get that feeling,
You know that it will last.

A special gift sent to us all,
Our hearts will beat as one;
But we will have to wait a while,
Until that day will come.

To be together and make a start,
Is every person's dream;
Everyone will know it's come,
Because your face will gleam.

To make it last is really hard,
Our work cut out to do;
But as I go to sleep at night,
I can only dream of you.

Lord

You're said to watch us up above,
So fill our hearts with tender love;
Let us be happy, and never feel down,
Let us not weep, a smile not a frown.

We pray to You Lord, keep us all safe,
Send evil away, and goodness awake;
Look after our health, and keep us all well,
Show others the light, who suffer and dwell.

Make us do good, with the things that we have,
Pick up the pieces, when we're feeling sad;
Wipe all the tears, and make a new start,
We pray to You Lord, keep open our hearts.

Let us all know, what's lying ahead,
Let us awake, when we sleep in our bed;
Make all our lives, be happy and gay,
We pray to You Lord, please show us the way.

The Ballerina

Tiptoeing across the dance floor,
She moves so lightly around;
With her fine and elegant movements,
Her feet hardly touching the ground.

Her elegant legs and white ballet shoes,
A silence she wears, every step that she moves;
Beautiful hands and fingers so long,
Not muttering a word, not even a song.

As we watch her dance her heart away,
Peaceful and happy, she'll dance and she'll sway;
Up in the air, her toes to the floor,
Spinning around, her eyes to the wall.

Flying through the air, as if like a bird,
Up to the skies, then back down to earth;
Amazing to watch, we look and we stare,
Oh, pure ballerina, with your long flowing hair.

The Frost

As I looked out the windowpane,
'Twas a night, the frost it came;
Glistening white upon the ground,
No creatures about, not even a sound.

Rubbing my hands, to keep them both warm,
Shining so white, all over our lawn;
Crispy and cold, it lies on the floor,
Upon the tree tops, and even our door.

Beautifully glistening, but ever so cold,
A mysterious thing, yet to unfold;
Slowly it goes, before our own eyes,
The frost melts away, the sun's in the skies.

Picking the Fruits

I remember when I was a little child,
We used to pick the fruits;
Carrying our baskets on the land,
Going to get our loots.

Strawberries, gooseberries and cherries too,
We'd fill our baskets, as high as the moon;
Pay at the cabin, then take them all home,
Make strawberry tarts and then cherry scones.

I remember those days, ever so clear,
Beautiful days, the summer was here;
Ate all the fruits, our tummies they ached,
Out with the medicine, after we'd baked.

Those childhood memories will always stay,
The birds were singing, and off on our way,
To the farm for a pick, and eat all we could,
Too full for our dinners, not even a pud.

Our Special Song

There always is a special song,
You learn throughout your years;
A song you hear, when you grow up,
To wipe away those tears.

I remember my dad would sing with me,
That song that I so loved;
He'd sit beside me on my bed,
And watch my face light up.

I'd sing the song along with him,
As loud as I could sing;
As I laugh now, as I look back,
It must have sounded a din.

For I never really knew the words,
As I was only three;
That childhood memory with my dad,
Will always stay with me.

Our tune, it is a special one,
We sang with so much fun;
Humming the tune along with Dad,
Called 'Seasons in the Sun'.

Our Special Love

I never will forget that day,
We took our vows for life;
I always will be proud of him,
Proud to be his wife.

Whenever I am feeling down,
He'll cuddle up to me;
He'll ease my pain and make me smile,
A brighter path I'll see.

We have a very special bond,
That no one could replace;
Nothing could describe our love,
You'll see it in our face.

As I look deep into his eyes,
I feel like I'm up high;
Through any troubles that we've had,
We'll both still touch the sky.

My perfect man, my perfect love,
I love with all my heart;
A doting dad, a friend to me,
Let God thee never part.

Dedicated to my husband, Nick.

The Short Life

To hold a few grudges, we must not do,
Smile every day, even when we are blue;
Make note of the lessons, we learn each day,
Guide all the people, who go the wrong way.

Life is too short, to live in such pain,
Life is too short, to be oh so vain;
Life is too short to quarrel and fight,
To live in the dark and not see the light.

Teach all of those, who cannot see wrong,
Help those that weep, cry only a song;
Help all the sufferers, as best as you can,
Ease all the pain, and all live with man.

Do all those things, that you only dreamed,
All of those goals, not as hard as they seem;
Give your support to the people who dwell,
Whisper only kind words, and never a yell.

For life is too short, for many a thing,
Let wars never come, but the birds always sing;
For tomorrow is brighter, than what we now see,
Open your hearts, let the sun shine on thee.

The Children's Riddle

Who made Pinocchio with the famous long nose?
Who follows Simba wherever he goes?
Who found Rudolph, with a nose oh so red?
Who kissed the Beauty, asleep in her bed?

Who cast the spell on the Princess so white?
Who made Cinderella dance with delight?
Who made Oliver, beg for some more?
Who made Dumbo, with ears to the floor?

Who was the Queen, turned envy and green?
Who let Pocahontas float up the stream?
Who made Mickey love Minnie so much?
Who made them all, with the magical touch?

Never a Doubt

They said our love would never last,
And now we've proved them wrong;
We've built a wall around our love,
A wall that is so strong.

Nothing in this whole wide world,
Could make our wall fall down;
For we know deep inside our hearts,
A love so rare we've found.

We always knew, we'd make it through,
The bad times and the sad;
We've come so far and yet to go,
The best we haven't had.

As we walk round, and hold a smile,
To those who had their doubt;
We've proved you wrong, we'll sing a song,
Our love is what we'll shout.